INSTRUMENTAL CD+ INSIDE PLAY-ALONG

POP & COU... INSTRUMENTAL...

GW00569833

Arranged by Bill Galliford
and Ethan Neuburg

udio recordings produced by
Dan Warner, Doug Emery,
and Lee Levin

CONTENTS

Title	Artist	Page	Demo	Play-Along
Tuning Note (B♭ Concert)				1
Shape of You	Ed Sheeran	2	2	3
Feel It Still	Portugal. The Man	4	4	5
How Long	Charlie Puth	6	6	7
There's Nothing Holdin' Me Back	Shawn Mendes	8	8	9
Attention	Charlie Puth	10	10	11
Say Something	Justin Timberlake (Featuring Chris Stapleton)	12	12	13
Believer	Imagine Dragons	14	14	15
Meant to Be	Bebe Rexha (Featuring Florida Georgia Line)	16	16	17
One Foot	Walk the Moon	18	18	19
Havana	Camila Cabello (Featuring Young Thug)	20	20	21
The Champion	Carrie Underwood (Featuring Ludacris)	22	22	23
Broken Halos	Chris Stapleton	23	24	25

mp3 CD Track

© 2018 Alfred Music
All Rights Reserved. Printed in USA.

ISBN-10: 1-4706-4090-2 (Book & CD)
ISBN-13: 978-1-4706-4090-3 (Book & CD)

Alfred

SHAPE OF YOU

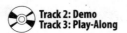

Track 2: Demo
Track 3: Play-Along

Words and Music by
KEVIN BRIGGS, KANDI BURRUSS,
TAMEKA COTTLE, ED SHEERAN,
JOHNNY McDAID and STEVE MAC

Shape of You - 2 - 1

Track 4: Demo
Track 5: Play-Along

FEEL IT STILL

Words and Music by
JOHN GOURLEY, ZACH CAROTHERS,
JASON SECHRIST, ERIC HOWK, KYLE O'QUIN,
JOHN HILL, ASA TACCONE, ROBERT BATEMAN,
GEORGIA DOBBINS, WILLIAM GARRETT,
FREDDIE GORMAN and BRIAN HOLLAND

Feel It Still - 2 - 1

HOW LONG

Track 6: Demo
Track 7: Play-Along

Words and Music by
CHARLIE PUTH, JUSTIN FRANKS
and JACOB HINDLIN

Moderate rock (♩ = 110)

How Long - 2 - 1

THERE'S NOTHING HOLDIN' ME BACK

Track 8: Demo
Track 9: Play-Along

Words and Music by
SCOTT FRIEDMAN, SHAWN MENDES, TEDDY GEIGER
and GEOFFREY ELLIOT WARBURTON

There's Nothing Holdin' Me Back - 2 - 1

Track 10: Demo
Track 11: Play-Along

ATTENTION

Words and Music by
CHARLIE PUTH and
JACOB KASHIR HINDLIN

Attention - 2 - 1

Track 12: Demo
Track 13: Play-Along

SAY SOMETHING

Words and Music by
CHRIS STAPLETON, MOWF DANJA,
LARRANCE DOPSON, TIMBALAND
and JUSTIN TIMBERLAKE

Say Something - 2 - 1

Track 14: Demo
Track 15: Play-Along

BELIEVER

Words and Music by
ZACHARY BARNETT, JAMES ADAM SHELLEY,
MATTHEW SANCHEZ, DAVID RUBLIN,
SHEP GOODMAN and AARON ACCETTA

Moderately (♩ = 120) (♫ = ♪³♪)

Believer - 2 - 1

15

Believer - 2 - 2

MEANT TO BE

Track 16: Demo
Track 17: Play-Along

Words and Music by
JOSH MILLER, TYLER HUBBARD,
DAVID GARCIA and BEBE REXHA

Meant to Be - 2 - 1

ONE FOOT

Track 18: Demo
Track 19: Play-Along

Words and Music by
BEN BERGER, RYAN MCMAHON,
RYAN RABIN, ELI MAIMAN,
NICHOLAS PETRICCA, KEVIN RAY
and SEAN WAUGAMAN

One Foot - 2 - 1

Track 20: Demo
Track 21: Play-Along

HAVANA

Words and Music by
BRIAN LEE, LOUIS BELL,
CAMILA CABELLO, FRANK DUKES,
BRITTANY HAZZARD, ALI TAMPOSI,
ANDREW WATT, YOUNG THUG
and PHARRELL WILLIAMS

Havana - 2 - 1

THE CHAMPION

Track 22: Demo
Track 23: Play-Along

Words and Music by
CARRIE UNDERWOOD, BRETT JAMES,
CHRISTOPHER BRIDGES and CHRIS DESTEFANO

Moderate rock (♩ = 91)

BROKEN HALOS

Track 24: Demo
Track 25: Play-Along

Words and Music by
CHRIS STAPLETON and MIKE HENDERSON

Moderately slow (♩ = 80)

PARTS OF A CLARINET AND FINGERING CHART

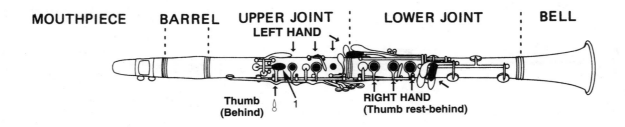

● = press the key or cover the hole with your finger.
○ = do not press the key or cover the hole.

When there is more than one fingering given for a note, use the first one unless the alternate fingering is suggested.

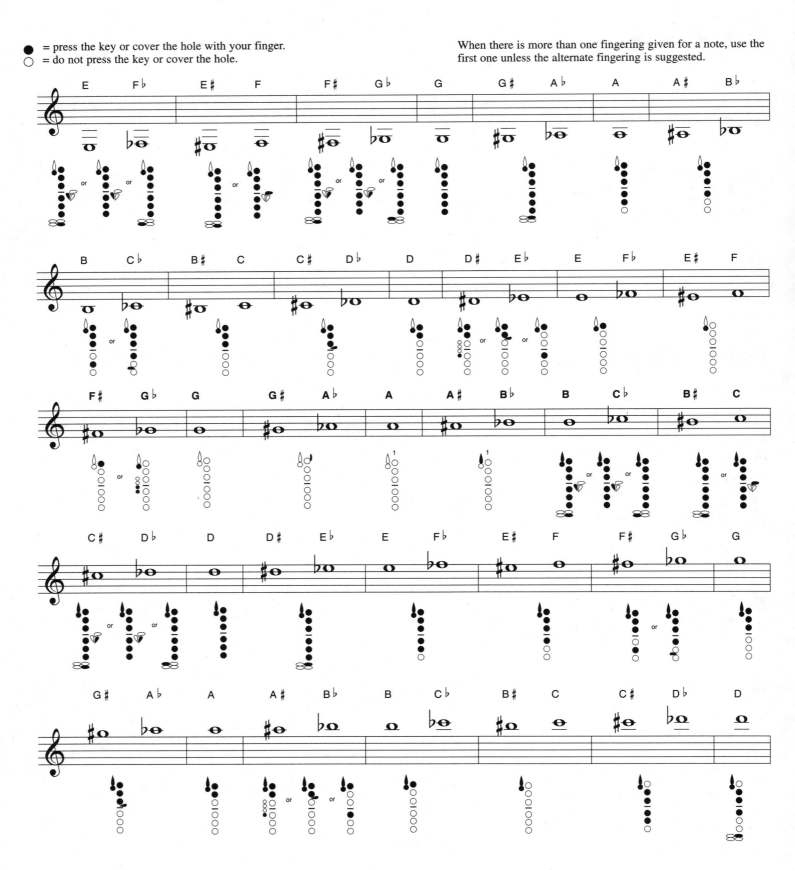